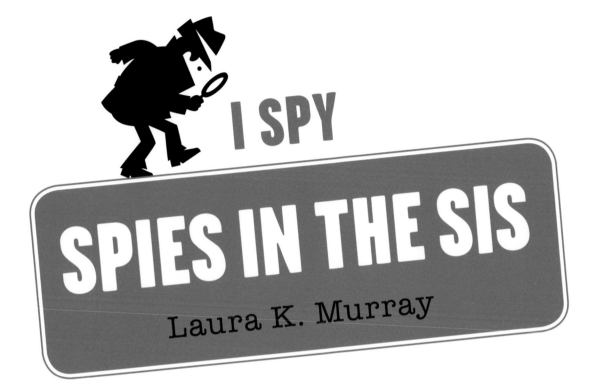

I SPY

SPIES IN THE SIS

Laura K. Murray

Creative Education ⊕ Creative Paperbacks

Published by Creative Education and Creative Paperbacks
P.O. Box 227, Mankato, Minnesota 56002
Creative Education and Creative Paperbacks
are imprints of **The Creative Company**
www.thecreativecompany.us

Design and production by **Christine Vanderbeek**
Art direction by **Rita Marshall**
Printed in the **United States of America**

Photographs by Corbis (Bettmann, KACPER PEMPEL/
Reuters, Science Photo Library, Tarker), Getty Images
(Apic, Thomas Backer, Arthur Schatz, KIRSTY WIGGLES-
WORTH, Greg Williams/Eon Productions), Shutterstock
(Alexandr III, BeRad, Milos Djapovic, SmileStudio, SoRad,
tele52)

Library of Congress Cataloging-in-Publication Data
Murray, Laura K.
Spies in the SIS / Laura K. Murray.
p. cm. — (I spy)
Includes index.
Summary: An early reader's guide to SIS spies, introducing
British espionage history, famous agents such as Christine
Granville, skills such as code making, and the dangers all
spies face.

ISBN 978-1-60818-619-8 (hardcover)
ISBN 978-1-62832-231-6 (pbk)
ISBN 978-1-56660-666-0 (eBook)
1. Intelligence—Great Britain—Juvenile literature. 2.
Espionage, British—Juvenile literature. 3. Spies—Great
Britain—Juvenile literature. 4. Great Britain. MI6—
Juvenile literature. I. Title.

JN329.I6M87 2015
327.1241—dc23   2014048721

CCSS: RI.1.1, 2, 3, 4, 5, 6, 7, 10; RI.2.1, 2, 3, 5, 6, 7; RI.3.1,
3, 5, 7; RF.1.1, 3, 4; RF.2.4

First Edition HC 9 8 7 6 5 4 3 2 1
First Edition PBK 9 8 7 6 5 4 3 2 1

TABLE OF CONTENTS

I SPY

A BRITISH SPY

THE NIGHT IS DARK. A BRITISH

secret agent cuts through the water in a fast boat. Then she slows down. She flashes a light off and on. She waits. A light blinks back from shore! The spy is using a code.

James Bond is a
made-up SIS agent.

Great Britain

SPIES WORK ALL OVER THE

world. They work in secret to gather information. In Great Britain, spies work for the SIS. This group began in 1909. Some people call it MI6.

BRITAIN HAS USED SPIES FOR

many years. Queen Elizabeth I hired spies in the 1500s. **World War II** spies broke German codes.

SECRETS AND CODES

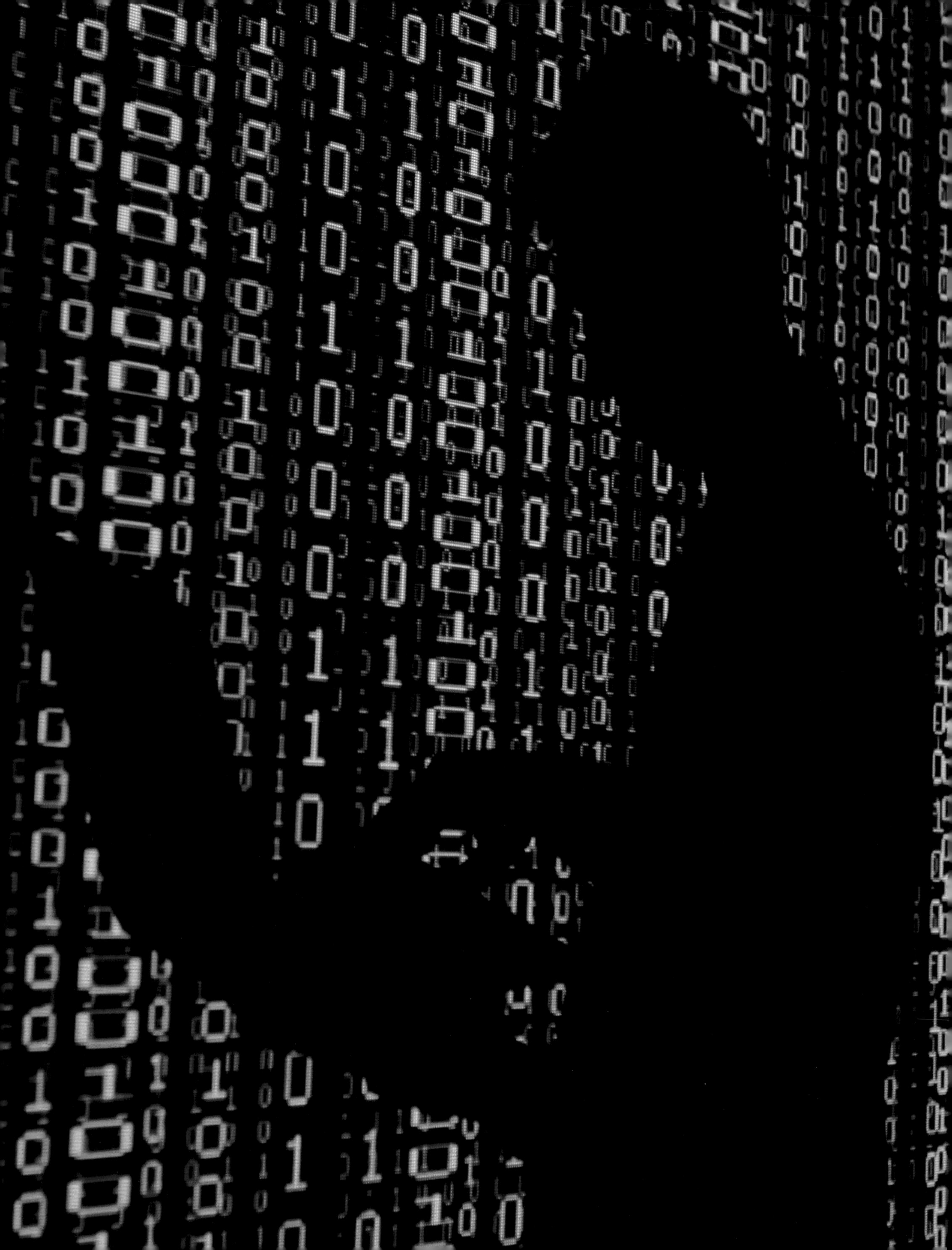

Computers can be
full of secrets.

SMART SPIES

SIS SPIES MUST BE SMART

and brave. Some spies know a
lot about computers. Others are
good at languages.

NEW AGENTS TRAIN IN

southern England. The spies learn how to work **undercover** and make codes. They train for six months or more.

CHRISTINE GRANVILLE WAS

born in Poland. She skied across mountains to spy for the British. She even jumped out of planes! She was caught a few times—but she always escaped.

GREAT ESCAPES

TOOLS AND TRICKS

Hidden objects called bugs pick up sound.

SIS SPIES HIDE MESSAGES IN

pens, coins, or rocks. Sometimes spies hook up special objects to phones. Then they listen in secret. This is called tapping.

A HARD JOB

IT IS NOT EASY BEING A SPY.

There are many people you cannot trust. Kim Philby worked in the SIS. But he was really a double agent for Russia.

THE SIS REPORTS TO

government leaders. Then spies get new jobs around the world. They get other people to help spy for Britain!

TOP-SECRET ACTIVITY

#9425: Be a Codebreaker

Spies use codes to talk in secret. Make your own spy code, and use it with a fellow spy!

Tools:
paper
pencil

Orders: Write out the letters of the alphabet on a piece of paper. Number the letters 1 through 26. For example, "A" will be "1," and "B" will be "2." Make a message with your code. ("8 9!" would mean "Hi!")

How could you use other numbers or pictures to make a code?

A = 1
B = 2
C = 3
D = _
E = _
F = _
G = _
H = _
I = _
J = _
K = _
L = _
M= _
N = _
O = _
P = _
Q = _
R = _
S = _
T = _
U = _
V = _
W= _
X = _
Y = _
Z = _

22

GLOSSARY

agent   someone who works as a spy

code   a system of letters or numbers that stand for other letters or numbers

double agent   a spy who pretends to work for one country while really working for another

undercover   working in secret and pretending to be someone else

World War II   the war between the Allied forces (like Britain) and the Axis forces (like Germany) that lasted from 1939 to 1945

READ MORE

Stewart, James. *Spies and Traitors*. North Mankato, Minn.: Smart Apple Media, 2008.

Walker, Kate, and Elaine Argaet. *So You Want to Be a Spy*. North Mankato, Minn.: Smart Apple Media, 2004.

WEBSITES

BBC HISTORY: CODE BREAKING
*http://www.bbc.co.uk/history
/code_breaking/*
Watch videos about British code-breakers during World War II.

INTERNATIONAL SPY MUSEUM: KIDSPY ZONE
*http://www.spymuseum.org
/education-programs/kids
-families/kidspy-zone/*
Play spy games, and learn how to talk like a secret agent.

Note: Every effort has been made to ensure that the websites listed above are suitable for children, that they have educational value, and that they contain no inappropriate material. However, because of the nature of the Internet, it is impossible to guarantee that these sites will remain active indefinitely or that their contents will not be altered.

INDEX